THE OFFICIAL GUIDE TO SNEAKY

Vol. I

F. Daniel Peak

www.officialsneaky.com

authorHOUSE™

1663 LIBERTY DRIVE, SUITE 200
BLOOMINGTON, INDIANA 47403
(800) 839-8640
WWW.AUTHORHOUSE.COM

First published by AuthorHouse 10/26/05

ISBN: 1-4208-8641-X (sc)

Library of Congress Control Number: 2005908912

Printed in the United States of America
Bloomington, Indiana

This book is printed on acid-free paper.

INTRODUCTION

Sneaky: (adj.) Marked by stealth, furtiveness, shiftiness; sly, secret (*Webster's Seventh New Collegiate Dictionary*)

The World is a sneaky place, and the exploration of all things sneaky is a fascinating one. I have been studying and observing all things sneaky since I was just a small lad. I have noticed sneakiness all around me, in all situations, circumstances and environments. Even before I was born, I had an innate sense of sneaky.

So, what is Sneaky? Is it something that is over-estimated . . . or under-estimated? Is it a profession that has special access to information about our lives that could be harmful or manipulated (such as a lawyer, an accountant, or an auditor)? What about a detour - how sneaky is that? We simply follow the detour signs blindly, not knowing where we're going or why.

How sneaky is a smile or smirk? We see these expressions all the time, but do we ever know what they really mean? Is sneaky something we never question, just because we're conditioned to accept (time zones!)

Perhaps this *Official Guide To Sneaky* will help you understand your world a little bit better - your sneaky world that it is . . .

a french corporation that doesn't
make anything
an ambulance driver - wakes up
in a dairy queen
a town in which even the people
who live there can't remember its
namc
yeah, i see
yeah i see - i see what you mean

– *Strange Ritual*
david byrne

This book is dedicated to (in sneaky alphabetical order by their last names):

- James Earl (Bo) Baker, III •
- David Byrne •
- David Cone •
- David Brown •
- Archibald Grubb •
- Q. R. Jones, Ph.D. •
- Mr. and Mrs. John M. Lee •
- Connie J. Peak •
- David Peak •
- Fred D. Peak •
- John Peak •
- Jason Williams, MD •
- Judson Worthy •
- Heineken USA, Inc. •

and especially to my beloved, beautiful, brilliant Muse, Elizabeth Taylor

1 • How sneaky is getting a second opinion?

Does it ever count?

2 • How sneaky is Leap Year?

And time, for that matter? How do we know that today is Tuesday? As a matter of fact, how sneaky is Tuesday?

3 • How sneaky is the fine print?

4 • How sneaky is + shipping and handling?

Why is this mentioned at the end of a commercial or order form? We never know how much something is really going to cost!

5 ● How sneaky are Extra Innings?

Do we just keep going until someone finally wins?

6 ● How sneaky is "90 days same as cash?"

What does that really mean – same as cash? What if there are complications on the 89th day?

7 ● How sneaky is the Bright Side?

How bright does that side need to be? And how long can one stay there?

8 ● How sneaky is a "Make Up Test?"

9 ● How sneaky is "the safe side?"

Should one consider the opportunity costs of playing it safe?

10 ● How sneaky is a satellite office?

Here today, gone tomorrow!

11 ● How sneaky is a money-back guarantee?

We hear it all the time, but do we ever use it?

12 ● How sneaky is a pop quiz?

13 ● How sneaky is the number 13?

Why is it unlucky? Why are there no 13th floors anywhere?

14 ● How sneaky is artificial flavoring

Why is it a benefit? Wouldn't everyone prefer real flavoring?

15 ● How sneaky is a third party?

And who invited them, anyway?

16 ● How sneaky is a Rebate?

Who really sends it in? And why are so many companies offering them rather than reducing the price outright? Because nobody sends them in.

17 • How sneaky is a substitute teacher?

How do we really know this is a teacher? What credentials are necessary to be a substitute teacher? Knowing how to read roll-call?

18 • How sneaky is a Non-Profit Organization?

Why don't they want to make money?

19 • How sneaky is "proof of purchase?"

Especially when one actually has the proof?

20 • How sneaky is a borrowed book?

Moreover, how sneaky is one who borrows a book and actually returns it?

21• How sneaky is a friend of the family?

"Oh, you can trust good old John with Margot. After all, he's a friend of the family!"

22• How sneaky is perfect attendance?

23• How sneaky is a limited partnership?

Does this protect the partners or the public? Or anything?

24• How sneaky is a Limited Offer?

Limited to whom? Who declares the sense of urgency? And for what reasons?

25● How sneaky is 'on second thought?'

What was so wrong with the first thought?

26● How sneaky is Chapter 13?

And what's the difference with Chapter 11? And who wants to read those chapters anyway?

27● How sneaky is the exchange rate?

28● How sneaky is White Out?

29 • How sneaky is a security deposit?

Security for whom? Where does the money actually go?

30 • How sneaky is trust?

A trust fund? A trusted friend? How far can one trust?

31 • How sneaky is the FDIC?

Does it really exist? Is it $100,000 per account or per individual? Confusing . . .

32 • How sneaky is wearing a medical ID bracelet?

33● How sneaky is 89 octane gasoline?

Does anyone actually buy it? When was the last time you bought it?

34● How sneaky is a two-way mirror?

Who is behind the two-way mirror watching . . .

35● How sneaky is a good patient?

How good does one need to be to qualify as a good patient? Never needing the nurse?

36● How sneaky is a chimney sweep?

Who chooses this profession . . . and why? (See "Mary Poppins")

37 • How sneaky is "starting the day out right?"

38 • How sneaky is a holding pattern?

What's the real reason? Will a holding pattern go on forever? What is the half life of a holding pattern?

39 • How sneaky is sticker price?

Who prices the sticker? Why can't we just have the price?

40 • How sneaky is a spare key?

And actually having one when you need it? Where is it?

41 • How sneaky is daylight savings time?

Since this saves time, how does it affect Leap Year?

42 • How sneaky is April 15th?

Who chose April 15th, in the middle of beautiful Spring, to cause ulcers?

43 • Who is the sneakiest person on "Gilligan's Island?"

Answer: The Professor!

44 • How sneaky is a spare tire?

And actually being fully prepared at all times and in all conditions to use it?

45 • How sneaky is the border?

46 • How sneaky is "Certain Restrictions Apply"?

What restrictions? And what happens if one doesn't follow them?

47 • How sneaky is Allan Greenspan?

What if he wakes up on the wrong side of the bed? By the way, how sneaky is the wrong side of the bed?

48 • How sneaky is the court recorder?

How do we know that we can trust the speedy typing to be completely accurate and not tainted by a late night – or hangover? After all, it is the official recording . . .

49● How sneaky is the Fifth Amendment?

50● How sneaky is 'a third wheel'?
Will the third wheel take your date and leave you without wheels?

51● How sneaky is a mid-life crisis?
Is it a reality, or an excuse?

52● How sneaky is page 13?

53 • How sneaky is a margin call?

Especially from your college roommate who is now a broker?

54 • How sneaky is a crawl space?

55 • How sneaky is the airport VIP lounge?

Who gets in? How good can an airport lounge actually be?

56 • How sneaky is a termite letter?

57 ● How sneaky is a park ranger?

58 ● How sneaky is Donald Duck orange juice?

Where does Donald make it? At Disney World?

59 ● How sneaky is a second date?

You still have to shower, you're still on your best behavior. And what is your best behavior?

60 ● How sneaky is the warning bell?

61 • How sneaky is a corporate seminar?

What is ever really accomplished other than staying in a nice hotel room – and how sneaky is room service?

62 • How sneaky is compound interest?

63 • How sneaky is calligraphy?

64 • How sneaky is spell check?

65 ● How sneaky is the state line?

Or the equator?

66 ● How sneaky is getting into something more comfortable?

A tease? An invitation? Or a bunny suit?

67 ● How sneaky is a preferred customer?

68 ● How sneaky is happy hour?

"Oh, don't worry, it's happy hour . . . is it stil hapie our?"

69 • How sneaky is being 99.9% sure?

Where is the .1%?

70 • How sneaky is a maiden name?

When does one use it? In politics?

71 • How sneaky is the eye of the hurricane?

And who wants to see it?

72 • How sneaky is Control-Alt-Delete?

This really solves all problems.

73 ● How sneaky is an out-of-court settlement?

And why is it always forgotten? And who really gets it?

74 ● How sneaky is "Plan B?"

Always be prepared!

75 ● How sneaky is a lamp shade?

Because it's more expensive than the lamp.

76 ● How sneaky is the "back burner?"

77 ● How sneaky is the fresh catch of the day?

Especially when the menu is pre-printed and the restaurant is 1,000 miles from the coast?

78 ● How sneaky is a lucky break?

And why is it broken?

79 ● How sneaky is "girls' night out?"

80 ● How sneaky is the space between the rock and a hard place?

81 ● How sneaky is time flying by?

Where does time actually go?

82 ● How sneaky is an all-you-can-eat-buffet?

83 ● How sneaky is a third base coach?

How is he selected? Where is third base, anyway?

84 ● How sneaky is an expert witness?

Who hires him? Why does the judge always accept an expert witness?

85 • How sneaky are Cliff Notes?

Where are they when we need them?

86 • How sneaky is an extension cord?

87 • How sneaky is a courtesy call?

Especially when it's automated . . .

88 • How sneaky is a haunted house?

Is it really real? Or do we all live in haunted houses?

89 ● How sneaky is a diagnosis?

90 ● How sneaky is a solar calculator?

Does one need to put it in the sun to work?

91 ● How sneaky is John - or Jane - Doe?

Do they ever get a real name?

92 ● How sneaky is a free consultation?

93 • How sneaky is an exclamation point?

94 • How sneaky is 'The State of the Union?'

Which state? Can this really be stated in thirty-minutes??

95 • How sneaky is a crossing guard?

Does this work only around schools? And, what authority do they really have?

96 • How sneaky is a Kodak moment?

And why does it always make us cry?

97● How sneaky is a #2 pencil?

What would happen if you used a #1?

98● How sneaky are the Hardy Boys?

And did they ever do anything wrong?

99● How sneaky is a Bookmobile?

And when does it come back so you can return your book?

100 ● How sneaky is college-ruled paper?

And why is it only mentioned before college?

101 ● How sneaky is "beating the crowd?"

102 ● How sneaky is a good faith estimate?

Why not just an estimate?

103 ● How sneaky is the "home field advantage?"

104 ● How sneaky is a white flag of surrender?

Isn't all fair in love and war?

105 ● How sneaky is the Geneva Convention?

Many sign, few follow.

106 ● How sneaky are the whole nine yards?

Who's yard?

107 ● How sneaky is the root of the problem?

Was it worth all the effort to dig that deeply?

108 ● How sneaky is the Surgeon General?

Who is he? What's his job – besides warnings on cigarette packs?

109 ● How sneaky is making a long story short?
Why delete the details?

110 ● How sneaky is lead-based paint?

111 ● How sneaky is silent investor?
What is he, a mime?

112 ● How sneaky is not tomorrow, not the next day, but the next day?

113 ● How sneaky was the Louisiana Purchase?

Was 3/4 of the US on sale that day?

114 ● How sneaky is a passing thought?

And how fast does it pass? In fact, this book almost passed!

115 ● How sneaky is the ADA?

And why can't we buy toothpaste without it's approval?

116 ● How sneaky is a curb appeal?

How appealing can a curb be? And why does it help sell a home?

117 • How sneaky is a reversible jacket?

Is this for one who has two dates in one night? Or were they made just for the 70s?

118 • How sneaky is the Prime Meridian?

How was it chosen to determine all other longitudes east and west?

Why is it in England?

119 • How sneaky is π?

120 • How sneaky is getting along?

121 ● How sneaky is an internal memo?
What happens if it's gets outside?

122 ● How sneaky is an all-inclusive vacation?

123 ● How sneaky is hotel honor bar?
Especially at 2:00 a.m.

124 ● How sneaky is a snow day?

125 ● How sneaky are flash cards?

126 ● How sneaky is a leaf collection?

127 ● How sneaky is going through a stage?

You can blame everything on that!

128 ● How sneaky is Pandora's Box?

Has it been opened lately? Can it be closed?

129 • How sneaky is a stopping point?

Does it ever start again?

130 • How sneaky is the long run?

How does one know when one's there?

131 • How sneaky is a dimmer switch?

132 • How sneaky is a sand bar?

133 • How sneaky is a combination lock?

Whocanrememberthecombination? Are these lock companies in cahoots with bolt cutter manufacturers?

134 • How sneaky is the bottom line?

135 • How sneaky is the Periodic Table?

136 • How sneaky is a ranger tower?

Do they really scan the horizons for fire? Or do they really just take a nap?

137 • How sneaky is a safety line?
Can you really trust whomever is holding it?

138 • How sneaky is the mailman?

139 • How sneaky is the "path less traveled?"

140 • How sneaky is a clown?

141 ● How sneaky is a 401K?

142 ● How sneaky is a dress rehearsal?

143 ● How sneaky is above average?
Who determines average?

144 ● How sneaky is a consultant?

145 ● How sneaky is a service light on your car?

How much will it cost to turn it off?

146 ● How sneaky is "requesting a window seat" on an airplane?

147 ● How sneaky is duty free?

Whose duty is it to make it free?

148 ● How sneaky is a Prime Number?

Is it better than any other number because it's Prime?

149 • How sneaky is an automatic bank draft?

150 • How sneaky is the telephone repair man?

151 • How sneaky is a disclaimer?

152 • How sneaky is a pinch hitter?

153 • How sneaky is a pre-approved loan?

154 • How sneaky is the line you must not cross?

"You children better not cross that line!"

155 • How sneaky is a safety deposit box?

156 • How sneaky is "one-of-a-kind?"

157 • How sneaky is free delivery?

158 • How sneaky is "plus or minus
_____?"

159 • How sneaky is a reduced
sentence?

160 • How sneaky is non-verbal
communication?

156 ● How sneaky is a deductible?

157 ● How sneaky is a confession?

284 ● How sneaky is a mime?

159 ● How sneaky is a second interview?

And how many more have to follow?

161 • How sneaky is a "good night's rest?"

162 • How sneaky is burning the midnight oil?

And how can you get a good night's rest if you do?

163 • How sneaky is minimum bet?

164 • How sneaky is "putting your mind to it?"

165 ● How sneaky is "elbow grease?"

166 ● How sneaky is a loose cannon?

167 ● How sneaky is a period?

168 ● How sneaky is a black hole?

169 • How sneaky is a lighthouse keeper?

170 • How sneaky is a House of Mirrors?

171 • How sneaky is a surge protector?

172 • How sneaky is extra credit?

173 ● How sneaky is a verbal contract?

174 ● How sneaky is overdrive?

175 ● How sneaky are jumper cables?

176 ● How sneaky is a family portrait?

177 ● How sneaky is a night light?

178 ● How sneaky is the jet stream?

179 ● How sneaky is a notary public?

180 ● How sneaky is a citizen's arrest?

181 ● How sneaky is a weatherman?

182 ● How sneaky is a local anesthetic?

183 ● How sneaky is a librarian?

184 ● How sneaky is "lifetime warranty?"

Your's or the corporation's?

185 • How sneaky is an official statement?

Does an official statement really carry so much more weight than any other statement?

186 • How sneaky is recess?

187 • How sneaky is dry cleaning?

188 • How sneaky is a fabric softener?

189 ● How sneaky is a check list?

190 ● How sneaky is a gifted child?

191 ● How sneaky is a Silicon Valley?

192 ● How sneaky is an exponential?

And who remembers what that means?

193 ● How sneaky is a station wagon? *Especially a Buick Roadmaster Estate Wagon?*

194 ● How sneaky is moss?

195 ● How sneaky is make-up?

196 ● How sneaky is a secret hiding place?

197 ● How sneaky is a door-to-door salesman?

198 ● How sneaky is a career track?

199 ● How sneaky is a feeling of belonging?

200 ● How sneaky is Braille?

201 • How sneaky is a manual typewriter?

202 • How sneaky is group mentality?

203 • How sneaky is the primary beneficiary?

204 • How sneaky is getting to something 'sooner or later'?

For example, this book!

205 ● How sneaky is the Nth degree?

206 ● How sneaky is gravity?

207 ● How sneaky is a daybed?

208 ● How sneaky is an extra ticket?

209 ● How sneaky is crop rotation?
Is this man versus nature?

210 ● How sneaky is 'off the record'?

211 ● How sneaky is cryptography?

212 ● How sneaky are phonetics?

213 ● How sneaky is a bright future?

214 ● How sneaky is "going by the house?"

215 ● How sneaky is the calm before the storm?

216 ● How sneaky is something that is "fairly new?"

217 • How sneaky is being "fairly certain?"

218 • How sneaky is staying neutral? *What's the point?*

219 • How sneaky is a bright idea?

220 • How sneaky is sticking to the original plan?

221 ● How sneaky is a nine iron?
Because it's almost a wedge.

222 ● How sneaky is the pick of the litter?

223 ● How sneaky is a chiropractor?

224 ● How sneaky is time and a half?

225 • How sneaky is an aptitude test?

226 • How sneaky is binding arbitration?

227 • How sneaky are occasional gusts?

228 • How sneaky is an off-shore bank account?

229 • How sneaky is a fork in the road?

230 • How sneaky is cruise control?

231 • How sneaky are Indian Reservations?

232 • How sneaky is a weigh station?

233 • How sneaky is a submarine?

234 • How sneaky is an undeclared dividend?

235 • How sneaky is "for old time's sake"?

236 • How sneaky is "touching base" with someone?

237 • How sneaky is "resume safe speed"?

238 • How sneaky is tag applied for . . .?

239 • How sneaky is "'Everybody, check under the bed"?

240 • How sneaky is something's "shelf life"?

241 ● How sneaky is a yield sign?

242 ● How sneaky is doing something on a whim?

243 ● How sneaky is a Philips head screwdriver

   Or having one?

244 ● How sneaky is a paper trail?

   Remember the Rose Law Firm, Little Rock, Arkansas?

245 ● How sneaky is a storm cellar?

246 ● How sneaky is solar power?

247 ● How sneaky is a corporate lobbyist?

248 ● How sneaky is self publishing?

249 • How sneaky is a cubic zirconia?
"I gave her a zirconia, and she'll think it's a diamond!

250 • How sneaky is the Mason-Dixon line?

251 • How sneaky is a gavel?

252 • How sneaky is a bow tie?

253 ● How sneaky is upward communication?

254 ● How sneaky is a pocket door?

255 ● How sneaky is a refrigerator magnet?

256 ● How sneaky is a password?

257 • How sneaky is a roundabout, especially in the United States?

258 • How sneaky is a Capri Sun?

259 • How sneaky is "at the appropriate time?"

260 • How sneaky is anger management?

261 • How sneaky is Sacramento, California?

262 • How sneaky is Tab?

263 • How sneaky is the Christmas spirit?

264 • How sneaky is Flag Day?

265 ● How sneaky is a church bus

266 ● How sneaky is an annulment?

267 ● How sneaky is a pet parade?

268 ● How sneaky is a benign tumor?

269 ● How sneaky is a coin collection

270 ● How sneaky is a gas lantern?

271 ● How sneaky is the Iowa Caucus?

272 ● How sneaky are the hiccups?

268 • How sneaky is a reflection?

269 • How sneaky is a dumb waiter?

270 • How sneaky is Carl Kasell of NPR?

271 • How sneaky is Columbus, GA?

Not as sneaky as Emily Shown

273 ● How sneaky is an icon?

274 ● How sneaky is Vacation Bible School?

275 ● How sneaky is a satellite?

276 ● How sneaky is Bertis Downs?

277 • How sneaky is a safety chute?

278 • How sneaky is "up to no good"?

279 • How sneaky is soil creep?

280 • How sneaky is plastic surgery?

281 ● How sneaky is human nature?

282 ● How sneaky is asking for advice?

283 ● How sneaky is Polaroid Picture?

284 ● How sneaky is Trapper Keeper?

285 • How sneaky is a Constable?

286 • How sneaky is a cyclone fence?

287 • How sneaky is a cottage industry?

288 • How sneaky is collateral?

289 ● How sneaky is Sarah Lee™?

290 ● How sneaky is roof flashing?

291 ● How sneaky is a highlighter?

292 ● How sneaky is an invisible ink pen?

293 • How sneaky is dry ice?

294 • How sneaky is FOB?

295 • How sneaky is an island-hopper?

296 • How sneaky is an infinity pool?

297 ● How sneaky is a Warranty Deed?

Does it belong to you or the bank?

298 ● How sneaky is ROM vs. RAM?

299 ● How sneaky is the Goodyear Blimp™?

300 ● How sneaky is having an umbrella?

301 ● How sneaky is a test flight?

302 ● How sneaky is sightseeing?

303 ● How sneaky is chit-chat?

304 ● How sneaky is a quarter tank of gas?

305 • How sneaky is "doing your best"?

306 • How sneaky is "no comment"?

307 • How sneaky is guide wire?

308 • How sneaky are record companies?

309 ● How sneaky is pre-fab construction?

310 ● How sneaky is the mall?

311 ● How sneaky is a drug store?

312 ● How sneaky is David Byrne?

313 • How sneaky are official guide books?

314 • How sneaky is a scout master?

315 • How sneaky is a carpet sweeper?

316 • How sneaky is a sneeze shield?

317 • How sneaky are royalties?

317 • How sneaky is the tooth fairy?

319 • How sneaky is a five o'clock shadow at 3:30 p.m.?

320 • How sneaky is a purchased royal title?

321 ● How sneaky are black-out curtains?

322 ● How sneaky is a craving?

323 ● How sneaky is a vacation spot?

324 ● How sneaky are God Parents?

325 • How sneaky is non-alcoholic beer?

326 • How sneaky are Roman Numerals?

327 • How sneaky is an adjustable rate?

328 • How sneaky is bookmark?

320 • How sneaky is a second chance?

330 • How sneaky is an out-patient procedure?

331 • How sneaky is Boxing Day?

332 • How sneaky is a smoke-filled room in Amsterdam . . .?

333 • How sneaky are reading glasses?

334 • How sneaky are the Twelve Days of Christmas?

335 • How sneaky is the heat index?

336 • How sneaky are nerds?

337 ● How sneaky is a guy named 'Bud'?

338 ● How sneaky is an in-box?

339 ● How sneaky is AB negative blood type?

340 ● How sneaky is a retaining wall?

341 • How sneaky are unfiltered cigarettes?

342 • How sneaky is a well-maintained aquarium?

343 • How sneaky is coozie?

344 • How sneaky is an electric pencil sharpener?

345 • How sneaky is a recipe?

346 • How sneaky is chlorophyll?

347 • How sneaky is keeping a diary?

348 • How sneaky is a graduated cylinder?

349 • How sneaky is a WATTS line?

350 • How sneaky is a tennis bracelet?

351 • How sneaky is a 9 volt battery?

352 • How sneaky is are Sperry Topsiders™?

353 • How sneaky is an alternator?

354 • How sneaky is an honorary degree?

355 • How sneaky is a Presidential Pardon?

356 • How sneaky is a team player?

357 • How sneaky is a trade show?

358 • How sneaky is "letting the dust settle?"

359 • How sneaky is homestead exemption?

360 • How sneaky is The Patriot Act?

361 • How sneaky is turning over a new leaf?

362 • How sneaky is a 4 way stop?

363 • How sneaky is a fuse?

364 • How sneaky is a first draft?

365 • How sneaky is Dramamine?

366 • How sneaky is the long run?

367 • How sneaky is a scribe?

368 • How sneaky are minor chords?

369 • How sneaky a Thesaurus?

370 • How sneaky is gravity?

371 • How sneaky is *Robert's Rules of Order*?

372 • How sneaky is the Dewey Decimal System?

373 • How sneaky is ground beef?

374 • How sneaky is a safety latch?

375 • How sneaky is a library card?

376 • How sneaky is an open book test?

377 ● How sneaky is DNA?

378 ● How sneaky is another round?

379 ● How sneaky is rocket science?

380 ● How sneaky is Phil Lesh?

381 • How sneaky are antioxidants?

382 • How sneaky is a blood pressure test result (179/69)?

383 • How sneaky is a 1031 tax exchange?

384 • How sneaky is the District of Columbia?

385 • How sneaky is "six degrees of separation?"

386 • How sneaky is stealth technology?

387 • How sneaky is a caboose?

388 • How sneaky is "a shoulder to cry on?"

389 • How sneaky is Tonto?

390 • How sneaky is the hundred year flood plain?

391 • How sneaky is the last laugh?

392 • How sneaky is being "behind the eight ball?"

393 ● How sneaky is a marsupial?

394 ● How sneaky is an escalator?

395 ● How sneaky is a misprint?

396 ● How sneaky is an air filter?

397 • How sneaky is rocket science?

398 • How sneaky is inventory?

399 • How sneaky are re-chargable batteries?

400 • How sneaky is the mercury in a thermometer?

401 • How sneaky is a medicine cabinet?

402 • How sneaky is a Sunday date?

403 • How sneaky is counterpoint?

404 • How sneaky is the American Stock Exchange?

405 • How sneaky is the right to remain silent?

406 • How sneaky is an honorable mention?

407 • How sneaky is _____?

408 • How sneaky is _____?

409 • How sneaky is _____?

410 • How sneaky is _____?

411 • How sneaky is _____?

412 • How sneaky is _____?

413 ● How sneaky is _____?

414 ● How sneaky is _____?

415 ● How sneaky is _____?

416 ● How sneaky is _____?

417 ● How sneaky is _____?

418 ● How sneaky is _____?

419 ● How sneaky is _____?

420 ● How sneaky is _____?

421 • How sneaky is _____?

422 • How sneaky is _____?

423 • How sneaky is _____?

424 • How sneaky is _____?

425 ● How sneaky is _____?

426 ● How sneaky is _____?

427 ● How sneaky is _____?

428 ● How sneaky is _____?

429 ● How sneaky is _____?

430 ● How sneaky is _____?

431 ● How sneaky is _____?

432 ● How sneaky is _____?

433 ● What do you consider sneaky? Please visit . . .
www.officialsneaky.com

Made in the USA
Lexington, KY
12 December 2010